THE BATTLING BIGHORNS

Lynn M. Stone

THE ROURKE CORPORATION, INC.
Vero Beach, FL 32964

Photo Credits:

© 1991 The Rourke Corporation, Inc.

Library of Congress Cataloging in Publication Data

Stone, Lynn M.
    The battling bighorns / by Lynn M. Stone
      p. cm. – (Animal odysseys)

    Includes index.
    Summary: Describes the physical characteristics,
habitat, and behavior of the Rocky Mountain Bighorn
sheep.
    ISBN 0-86593-107-0
    1. Bighorn sheep – Juvenile literature. 2. Bighorn
sheep – Rocky Mountains – Juvenile literature.
[1. Bighorn sheep. 2. Sheep.] I. Title. II. Series: Stone,
Lynn M. Animal odysseys.
QL737.U53S7435 1991
599.73'58–dc20

                         90-45991
                            CIP
                              AC

CONTENTS

1 ROCKY MOUNTAIN BIGHORNS

The magnificent curled horns worn by a Rocky Mountain bighorn ram are not mere decorations. The horns are weapons used by the bighorn ram to butt and brawl. His thick horns are battle-scarred and often splintered at their tips from clashes with other rams. His nose is lumpy and bruised, and it has probably been cracked a time or two. Dark and square-shaped, the Rocky Mountain ram looks like he

Left:
Dark and square-shaped, a Rocky Mountain bighorn ram looks like he was chiseled from high country rocks.

Right:
A bighorn's feet are like a fighter's feet – nimble and quick.

was chiseled from high country rocks for the sole purpose of fighting in mountain arenas.

A Rocky Mountain ram has a fighter's build, and he also has a fighter's feet – nimble and quick. Both rams and **ewes**, female bighorns, can perform dazzling feats of balance. In its high country home, the bighorn is a master of mountaineering. It bounds from ledge to ledge and runs with sure feet on rocky slopes.

Bighorns don't spend all of their energy butting and bounding. Although they are wild mountain sheep, they are closely related to **domestic**, or farm, sheep. As you know, farm sheep are animals of leisure. They spend

Left:
A young bighorn ram takes an afternoon rest to chew its cud in the Rockies of Montana.

Below:
These domestic Orkney rams are descendants of wild mountain sheep.

most of their time in flocks, grazing and resting. Although bighorns are more active than their cousins on the farm, they too spend a great amount of time in flocks, or bands, feeding on mountain grass, resting, and chewing their **cuds**.

Like domestic sheep, bighorns can be quite unafraid of people. In areas where they are not hunted, bighorns lose their fear of people and become tame easily. Bighorns in North American national parks, such as Banff and Jasper in Alberta, Canada, frequently feed along the highway shoulders. Sheep like these become

accustomed to people, and people on foot can often get quite close to them. Sometimes these bighorns simply ignore people, as if they have more important things to do, such as chewing their cuds. But they may also show curiosity, especially if they associate someone with food handouts.

Sheep have a taste for salt, and researcher Valerius Geist reported that mountain sheep will accept a person offering salt as a "two-legged salt lick if he so wishes." Geist found that the bighorns he fed could become a nuisance. In their efforts to find salt, they frequently stuck their noses into his jacket, tugged on his packboard, and licked his camera lens. Geist fed salt to these wild mountain sheep as part of a carefully controlled study of bighorns. Normally, no one should attempt to feed bighorns, because their behavior is unpredictable. They can become dangerous at any time, and Geist found that old rams occasionally became aggressive toward him when they did not get what they wanted right away.

Like many large grazing animals, bighorns have hooves, horns, and a digestive system that produces a cud to chew. Bighorns and other sheep differ somewhat from their relatives, which include cattle, bison, buffalo, goats, and antelope. The bighorn's closest relatives are goats. There are many similarities between sheep and goats, but male sheep have large curled or spiral horns that look like a screw's thread. Male goats have straighter,

Above:

Goats are the closest relatives of mountain sheep. This North American mountain goat is actually a goat-antelope.

more slender horns than rams. They also have beards, which rams do not. The horns and beards help set sheep and goats apart. **Biologists**, the people who study sheep and other living things, note that sheep and goats also have different arrangements of **glands**. Glands are body structures that contain and sometimes release a fluid of one kind or another. Sweat glands are among the best known human glands. Goats have a scent-producing gland at the base of their tails, but sheep do not. Although that difference in glands doesn't sound very important, it is one of the ways a scientist separates one group of animals from another.

9

Left:

Dall's sheep closely resemble bighorns, but their horns are wider and thinner.

Bighorns live in a harsh, rugged **environment** throughout the year. Their home is among the high peaks, meadows, and valleys of the Western mountains of North America. Not all of the world's seven **species**, or kinds, of mountain sheep live in such difficult terrain. The mountain sheep of Asia and Europe tend to live in hilly country rather than mountainous areas.

The bighorn *(Ovis canadensis)* and Dall's sheep *(Ovis dalli)* are the two North American species of

Right:

The desert bighorns of the Southwest differ slightly from their darker, larger relatives of the Rocky Mountains.

11

mountain sheep. Dall's sheep, which live in Alaska, are sometimes called "thinhorn" sheep. Dall's sheep look much like a white bighorn, but Dall's sheep horns are thinner and not as tightly curled as a bighorn's. Another "thinhorn," the Stone's sheep *(Ovis dalli stonei)*, is a Canadian version of the Dall's sheep. Stone's sheep live in northern British Columbia and the Yukon Territory. They can be largely black, silver gray, or a mix of those colors.

Bighorn sheep also vary in size and color. Generally, the bighorns of the Rocky Mountains are larger and darker than the bighorns of California and the Southwest. Biologists consider the differences among wild bighorns to be slight. Nevertheless, each of the different groups is considered a separate **race**. That simply means that each group has certain characteristics that separate it from the other groups. Most of these characteristic differences are slight, and biologists rarely agree on how many races of bighorn actually exist. Many biologists recognize five races – three types of desert bighorns, the California bighorn, and the Rocky Mountain bighorn, the subject of this book.

The Rocky Mountain bighorn is the largest of the clan. A ram may stand three and one-half feet tall at the shoulder, measure up to six feet long, and weigh 300 pounds. An extremely large ram can exceed 300 pounds. The female Rocky Mountain bighorn stands up to three feet tall at the shoulder and may measure more than five feet long. Rocky Mountain ewes are much slimmer than rams, weighing from 125 to 200 pounds.

Rocky Mountain sheep are the darkest of the bighorns. They are mostly brown with white patches behind their legs, on the belly, and on the rump. Their tails are dark and very short. Bighorns of the desert mountains are usually lighter than their northern relatives.

Life in the Rockies presents many hazards for the sheep. Bighorns face severe weather and occasional **predators**, like mountain lions and wolves. A sheep's alertness, keen sense of smell, and excellent eyesight help it react quickly to predators. The bighorn's ability to run short distances at high speed and take refuge on frighteningly rocky slopes and ledges usually takes it out of harm's way.

Part of the mountain sheep's agility on the slopes can be traced to its sharp hooves. The hooves have a rigid outer edge and a spongelike center. Because the hoof centers grip rocks, they give the sheep firm footing.

2 AT HOME IN THE ROCKY MOUNTAINS

Below:
*The Rocky
Mountain
bighorn's home
is a world of
high ridges
and alpine
meadows.*

The home of the Rocky Mountain bighorn is a world of spectacular high country. Dizzying heights and snow-clad peaks look down on **alpine** meadows, rock-tossed

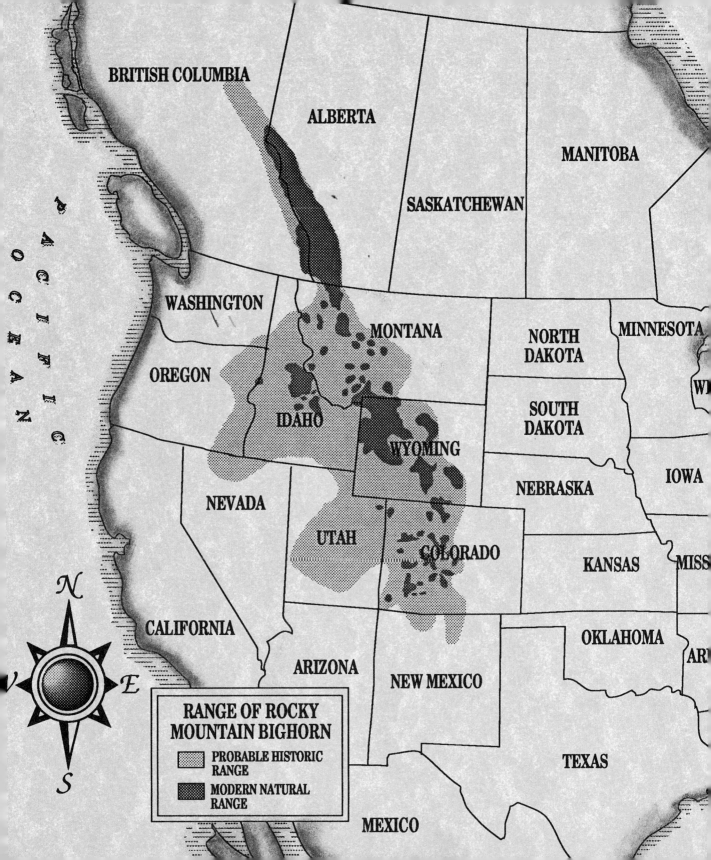

slopes, and green valleys. Cliffs drop off sharply, and gurgling brooks race downhill in **cascades**. When the sun sets on a clear evening, the snowy peaks glow in gold. But winds howl in the high country like wolves, and raging snow squalls may plaster the heights and mountain passes at almost any time of year. The ruggedly grand country to which these mountain sheep are suited can be extremely harsh.

The mountains are especially harsh in winter. Bighorns are among the few animals that remain in the mountains throughout the seasons. Most of the animals that share the bighorns' lofty home have found ways to

Above:
Marmots share the alpine heights with bighorns in the summer but disappear into their burrows to sleep winter away.

16

escape the worst of seasons. Grizzly bears, marmots, pikas, and ground squirrels, for example, crawl into dens and sleep winter away in **hibernation**. Ptarmigan, the wild chickenlike birds that turn white in the winter, live in sheltered tunnels under the snow. Mule deer and elk retreat to lower pastures. Rocky Mountain bighorns generally move downhill, too, but not too far. They often spend winter at surprisingly high **altitudes**, or heights.

Below:

Deep snow sometimes forces bighorns to feed on brush.

A bighorn's first defense against winter is its coat. It wears an outer coat of long, stiff hairs. Beneath them

is a warm, dense covering of underhair. (When warm weather arrives, bighorns **molt**, losing their outer coat in scruffy patches.) Bighorns also combat winter by having an abundance of fat from their late summer and autumn feeding. In addition, bighorns seek the warmest levels of mountain air. Curiously, the warmest air is not always at the lowest level.

Bighorns do not occupy all the mountain country of the Rockies. Actually, one herd of bighorns may be several miles from the next herd. In the southern Rockies especially, bighorn herds are widely scattered.

Rocky Mountain bighorn country extends from southwestern Alberta, Canada, south through the Rockies chains to southern Colorado. In the hundreds of miles between those two points, Rocky Mountain bighorns live in Montana, Idaho, Wyoming, and a corner of Utah. Other races of bighorns are found in the mountains of southern British Columbia, California, Arizona, New Mexico, Nevada, and northwestern Mexico.

Within the Rockies, bighorns have their own favorite type of land. This is called their **habitat**. The Rockies are studded with great forests of evergreen trees, but bighorns are not forest dwellers. Bighorn habitat is open ground, particularly mountain meadows and grassy hills near rocky cliffs. The grass is for eating, and the cliffs are for refuge. High country that has been opened by forest fires or avalanches is also appealing to bighorns.

3 SHEEP SOCIETY

In typical sheep fashion, bighorns are rarely alone. They are **gregarious**, which means they like each other's company and flock together. Throughout much of the year adult rams have their own bands, and ewes, lambs, and young rams form other bands. During the **rut**, the annual mating season, the rams mingle with the ewes and young sheep.

Right:
Bighorns are sociable animals, almost always traveling in each other's company.

The bands of bighorn sheep live on areas within their mountain habitat called home ranges. The sheep feed and sleep in the home range area and usually confine their daily wandering to it. The exact area used for a home range varies with the seasons. Winter ranges tend to be smaller than other seasonal ranges because the sheep's movements are limited by snow. In midwinter, bighorns may stay within a range no wider than one-half mile.

Bighorns change their range sites with the passing seasons. As winter approaches, they generally move downward to lower mountain heights. The range movement may be no more than from one mountain slope or

Below:
Bighorns spend winter on a range below their summer haunts.

valley to the next. Such travel is little more than a short hike. But some bighorns take off on a long journey, or **odyssey**, traveling up to 40 miles from one range to another.

These seasonal movements, regardless of their distance, are quite predictable. Year after year, at about the same time, a particular band of bighorns makes the same short **migration** from one place to another. Since the sexes are separate much of the year, bighorn rams and ewes follow somewhat different routes and schedules of travel. Nevertheless, all bighorns learn and follow **traditional** routes, routes which have been passed on from one generation of sheep to the next. Young sheep learn migration routes and ranges from their elders. Young ewes generally become part of the flock their mothers are in. When young rams move off to join bands of adult rams, they learn the routes and home ranges of the ram bands.

Still, there is some exchange of sheep between bands. Bighorns are very tolerant of each other. If a yearling ewe, for example, crosses paths with another band of ewes, she may join that group. In some cases, the young ewe may even wander after a ram and join the female band that his travels lead her to. Young sheep basically follow whatever adults they choose and become part of the adults' groups.

Bighorns become extremely attached to the routes and ranges they have learned, no matter what else may vie for their attention. Bighorn rams are keenly interested in ewes during the rut. On the journey to their traditional rutting range, however, rams may ignore flocks of ewes that are not on the rams' traditional range. This type of range loyalty works to keep bighorns from spreading and expanding their overall range. It also creates a problem for biologists and wildlife managers, the people who watch over preserves and work with wild animal populations. These people sometimes try to start new herds by transplanting bighorns into areas where there are no sheep. Faced with unfamiliar surroundings, the sheep are inclined to stay in a small area. They may quickly overgraze it and create unhealthy conditions for themselves. Despite their great ability to get around the mountains, they are poorly suited to be pioneers.

During seasonal journeys, young rams follow the **dominant**, or strongest, male. He is typically the ram with the largest horns. In turn, the bands of females and young sheep are led by an old ewe. Bands usually make five major moves in a year. The exact number depends on the particular herd, just as the number of bighorns in a band depends on a specific herd. Bighorns rarely travel in bands of less than five or more than fifty.

Above:

Smaller rams bow to the large, dominant ram to show their lower status in the group.

Rocky Mountain rams usually move to their autumn range in late September. Shortly afterward, they move to rutting grounds where they remain until the end of December. From the rutting range, they travel to a wintering site. In late March, on hard-packed snow, they journey to a late winter – early spring range where they can graze on patches of snow-free ground. In late June and early July the rams climb to their summer ranges.

23

4 LITTLE BIGHORNS

By May, spring is rapidly changing much of the white Rocky Mountain landscape to green. On south-facing slopes, wildflower blooms signal the passing of winter and the arrival of a new season. Bighorn ewes leave their winter range and trot single file to lambing areas.

Left:
Bighorn lambs are usually born in May.

Right:
Frolic and play are daily activities for bighorn lambs.

Usually a pregnant ewe leaves her band a week or two before having her lamb. She seeks a particularly rugged area among the cliffs. That lessens the chance of a predator finding and attacking the lamb.

The lamb weighs about eight pounds at birth and can walk within a few hours. The lamb is covered with a soft, woolly coat, and it already has two horn buds – knobs that eventually grow into full-size horns.

A ewe stays with her lamb at some distance from the other bighorns. The lamb rests, nurses, and plays, jumping and running about. After about a week away from the others, the ewe and her lamb return to the band of yearlings, two-year olds, and lambless ewes that remained together.

During the next week, each ewe watches her lamb carefully. A ewe may even butt another sheep that comes too close. A mother bighorn's attention to her lamb is short-lived, however. When a lamb is two weeks old, it has already begun to nibble on grass and explore. At this point, a ewe isn't concerned about her straying lamb, and the ewe's own feeding often takes her some distance away. Ewes, of course, return to their lambs from time to time to let them nurse.

The partnership between ewe and lamb weakens as the lamb grows older. Within the larger herd, lambs soon gather into their own bands. They run, frolic, and even begin to butt heads. By fall the youngsters are **weaned** – they no longer need or depend upon mother's milk. Now the ewes appear to have lost all interest in the lambs, and the lambs don't really need their mothers' attention anyway. The lambs have become seventy- and eighty-pound animals, and they are amazingly quick and agile as they dash about the highlands. The ewes still teach the lambs sheep behavior and travel routes, but they can't offer much protection to the lambs. Ewes' horns are slight and not very frightening. Ewes, like their lambs, depend on speed and footwork to avoid predators.

Young rams usually join bands of older males when they are two or three years old. They don't normally produce lambs of their own until they are six or seven. Meanwhile, young ewes usually have their first lamb at the age of three.

Rocky Mountain bighorns often live for more than ten years. Rams usually die sooner than ewes, and it is rare for either sex to reach the age of twenty.

5 HORNS

Bighorn rams are easily identified by their massive brown horns. Among the bighorn races, Rocky Mountain sheep have the biggest horns. By the time a Rocky Mountain ram is seven or eight, he may have horns whose tips sweep up to their bases. These are known as "full curl" horns. Old rams occasionally have curls beyond "full," but these horns tend to be broken and splintered at their tips, or **broomed**. Brooming may result from a ram's fights with other rams or from the horns being rubbed. Horns that are too curled block the ram's side vision. Then the animal shortens them by wearing them down against rocks.

Large Rocky Mountain rams have horns that sometimes reach forty-two inches in length. More often rams have horns about thirty-six inches long. The record horn for a Rocky Mountain bighorn is forty-nine and one-half inches long. Naturally, such impressive headwear adds to a ram's weight as well as his stature. A 250-pound ram may carry 33 pounds of that total weight in its horns and skull.

Young rams have short, slim horns that are almost identical to the half-curl horns of ewes. Each year, however, the ram's horns grow from the base. The growth creates rings that help biologists determine the approximate age of a ram.

Left:
The horns of a bighorn ram are permanent fixtures, unlike the antlers of elk and deer.

Unlike antlers, which are worn by elk and deer, horns are permanently attached to an animal's skull. Elk and deer discard their antlers each year and grow new ones. Horns are made up of a bone interior sheathed in **keratin**. Keratin is a hard, tough substance that is commonly known as "horn." In addition to being found in horns, keratin is found in claws and fingernails.

Rocky Mountain bighorns use their horns as weapons against each other, but rarely against other animals. Only if it were cornered would a bighorn be likely to butt another animal.

Because they are blunt, Rocky Mountain sheep horns are not designed to puncture and cut. The sharp, daggerlike horns of the bighorn's cousin, the mountain goat, are much more dangerous weapons.

A bighorn's headgear is as much **symbol** as weapon. A symbol is something that stands for something else. To other sheep, the horns of a ram represent that animal's strength and rank within the band. The larger the horns, the greater the ram's rank, or **status**.

6 PREDATOR AND PREY

Rocky Mountain bighorns are alert animals, always on the lookout for predators. In some parts of the Rockies, bighorn sheep may meet mountain lions, wolves, coyotes, grizzly bears, lynxes, bobcats, wolverines, or golden eagles. Any one of these predators can kill a bighorn lamb, and a few of them can kill larger sheep. Bighorns are rarely **prey**, or food, of mountain predators, however. The ewe's choice of a steep cliff for her birthing place usually keeps her lamb hidden and out of reach.

While lambs are rarely preyed upon, their parents are even less likely to be prey. The only predator with the blend of speed, strength, and rock-hopping skill necessary to catch a healthy adult bighorn is the mountain lion, also known as the catamount, puma, and cougar. But mountain lions, like the rest of the predators, almost always prey on lambs or bighorns that are old, sick, or injured.

As agile as bighorns are, they are not immune to injuries from falls and fights. Falls sometimes result in broken legs. A crippled bighorn can eat but it cannot run, and eventually it becomes prey for a predator.

Right:
The cougar or mountain lion is one of the few predators large enough to attack an adult bighorn.

31

Bighorns are much more likely to die from a fall, an avalanche, or disease than from **predation**. Several species of roundworms cause diseases in bighorns. One of the chief killers in some bands is lungworm.

Bighorns are **herbivores**, or plant eaters. Like other grazing animals, they live entirely on plants. They lack the usual weapons of hunting animals, claws and sharp teeth.

Bighorns live largely on grass, although they also eat a variety of other green, non-woody plants. Many of the plants they eat are dry and dust-covered. Remarkably, they are able to thrive on sparse, tough vegetation. Most other grazing animals cannot live on such meager plants, so bighorns generally have high, rocky meadows to themselves.

Rocky Mountain bighorns eat lush plants whenever they can, but the high mountain environment in which they live provides neither a long growing season nor an abundance of thick grass. Rocks, wind, cold, snow, and poor soil combine to produce rather skimpy gardens in the upper reaches of sheep country. Rocky Mountain bighorns in Yellowstone National Park and Rocky Mountain National Park, for example, can be found grazing on the dry, windswept mats of alpine tundra that cover the ground above **timberline**. Here in these mountain communities without trees, the grasses and leaves are wiry and thin.

Right:
*Bighorns live
on a diet of
plants, mostly
grasses.*

7 BATTLING BIGHORNS

The northern Rockies in late autumn are cold and bleak under gray skies. Yellowed spears of grass poke through a frosting of snow and shudder in the wind. The marmots, the plump whistlers of summer days, have retired to the warmth and protection of their dens. Gone too are the ground squirrels and little pikas. Like the marmots, they are underground, sleeping away autumn and winter to come. But the Rockies are far from lifeless. The mountain winds telegraph the crack of colliding horns and skulls. Bighorn rams, strong, sleek, and high-spirited, do battle.

Rocky Mountain rams may fight at any time. In late fall, however, at the beginning of the mating season, the likelihood of fights increases. Big rams unknown to each other often meet on the rutting range, and a ram does not greet a strange ram kindly. Rather, each ram sees another as a challenge to his standing within the group. Since a ram's standing within the band directs his life, a fight erupts.

Above:

A dominance fight may begin when one ram challenges another with a kick.

In his own band, a ram knows his place. Fighting and butting throughout the year establish an order, or rank, of dominance. By autumn the matter of who is toughest has been pretty well worked out. Each band has its "king of the mountain." The arrival of a new face or two on the rutting site can upset the ram's social order. If a strange ram is larger than the other rams, he is not challenged. If the new ram matches up in horns with another big ram, most often in the three-quarter curl size, the two will clash.

Rams grow up as fighters. Bighorn rams fight more than any other big North American grazing animals. Bison, mountain goats, pronghorns, elk, deer, and

35

moose limit their duels to one season. Bighorns fight throughout the seasons. A bighorn ram fights for control, or dominance, of the other rams. He does not fight for sport or exercise. Even after a leader of a band has emerged, younger, smaller-horned rams battle for position within the group. Most fighting among bighorns, in fact, takes place between five- to seven-year-old rams with three-quarter curls.

Typically, bighorns of the same size fight one another. They avoid mismatches. Through butting and shoving contests, bighorns learn how strong they are, and they don't waste energy on hopeless struggles with bigger sheep.

Below:
Dominance fights are tests of strength and endurance.

Most clashes between bighorns are true dominance battles. In these contests, bighorn rams rush at each other and strike each other's horns. One ram often jockeys for uphill position so that he can generate greater force than his opponent. The rams collide with a combined force of perhaps 40 miles per hour. The ringing sound of their head-on collisions drifts more than a mile in the wind.

Sometimes, like a bicycle riding upright on its rear wheel, the rams run at each other on hind legs. At other times they clash on all fours. The staggering force of the blow between their skulls can jerk their hind feet right off the battlefield.

The rams' energy for battle, once it has begun, can be almost unimaginable. They may fight for hours, neither ram giving quarter for long. Fights may be interrupted by time-outs to feed, and perhaps to let groggy heads clear, but both battlers resume their clash until one acts defeated. Valerius Geist, who studied North American mountain sheep in the wild for nearly four years, once watched a pair of mountain sheep in a twenty-five hour duel!

Fortunately for the losing ram, defeat doesn't mean death or even necessarily injury. Bighorn rams are built to take abuse from one another, which explains why they can fight for twenty-five hours and still be standing. The rams' secret is a heavy skull structured with a double layer of bonework. Their horns and heads absorb repeated blows quite easily despite the tremendous force involved. Seldom do they sustain major injuries. Nevertheless, there are minor scrapes and bruises. Hair is torn out from contact with the rough horns, cuts may appear around the nose and eyes, and the rams' ribs are sometimes broken. Head-on charges aren't likely to break ribs, of course, but fights between two rams seem to stir combat instincts in other rams. Occasionally a ram will charge from the sidelines and butt the shoulder or rib cage of one of the fighters.

A ram is defeated when he quits the battle. He doesn't collapse or run away. He simply stops fighting. He grazes and apparently signals a surrender of sorts by turning his white rump patch toward the victor. He also avoids any aggressive motions, such as kicking or butting. The winner, for his part, may continue to act aggressively by kicking the loser and showing that he is again ready to fight.

Being the biggest and strongest is not always in the ram's best interest. Studies of bighorns have shown that the most dominant rams may not live as long as the less dominant ones. It seems likely that the rams which fight most frequently have less fat, and therefore less energy, left for winter survival. Thus the dominant rams often live their lives faster, as well as harder, than the sheep they dominate.

Right:
Before turning his white rump patch to the victor, the loser (left) bows in submission.

The main benefit of being a dominant ram occurs during the mating season. The top-ranked ram, like a storybook hero, draws the ladies' attentions more easily than the other rams. And he can drive away smaller rams from any ewe that interests him. The dominant ram also finds that ewes prefer rams with large horns. Ewes often show total disinterest in smaller suitors.

There are exceptions, however. Sometimes when a dominant ram chases a ewe, he is hounded by another eager ram that hasn't learned its place in the rankings. The big ram will break off the chase long enough to whirl and attack his rival. The pause in the chase may give a third ram the chance to rush off with the ewe. Meanwhile, the fight may be especially brutal, leading to broken ribs or even legs. Fights over females aren't common, and they are rather sudden, no-holds-barred events. They differ from the pitched, head-on battles that mark dominance fights. When his courtship of a ewe is interrupted, a ram may turn with fury on its smaller rival and plow into its side or rump and knock it sprawling. The big ram may then rush to butt the fallen ram again.

Rams of various rank stay on the same range together during the rut. Rams do not have a patch of ground, or **territory**, to defend. Neither do they try to guard a flock of ewes. Therefore, once dominance battles have settled rank, conflict among rams in the band disappears, and they stay together. In contrast, a dominant bull elk guards several elk cows from other bulls. The bull keeps the cows together even before they are all ready to mate. A bighorn ram, however, is interested in a ewe only when she is ready to mate. Then a dominant ram will guard that one ewe for a short time before finding another.

Left:
A big ram, whose courtship of a ewe has been interrupted, turns viciously on a smaller ram.

8

SAVING THE BIGHORNS

The biggest battle waged by bighorns during the past 150 years has been the battle for survival. With the settlement of the American West, bighorns began to suffer from problems introduced by pioneers and their farm animals. Many of those problems still exist today.

As more and more people flocked into the home of the bighorns, large numbers of sheep were shot. Many of them were killed by market hunters, men who hunted wild animals to sell in the new country's growing meat business. The easternmost race of bighorns, the Audubon or Badlands bighorn, was hunted to **extinction**; it was completely wiped out. The bighorns in the South Dakota Badlands today are descendants of Rocky Mountain bighorns, which were transplanted to the Badlands. The California bighorn came dangerously close to extinction.

Hunting laws stopped the mass killing of mountain sheep many years ago. Hunters now need a license to hunt bighorns, and the sheep may only be hunted during a specific hunting season. Several western states and Canadian provinces offer hunting seasons on bighorns. The game departments of the states and provinces determine each year how many bighorns that hunters will be allowed to shoot.

Bighorn meat is tasty, but most hunters want the mountain sheep for their horns. Hunters usually target the largest rams. Unfortunately, taking the biggest rams deprives the flock of leadership and the strength that could be passed to future generations of sheep. Legal hunting, however, does not threaten the survival of the sheep. The bighorns' chief problems are not related to guns.

The bighorn has been most severely hurt by its domestic relative, the farm sheep. The number of domestic sheep grew in the nineteenth century as the West was settled. Domestic sheep ate grass cover that, in some high places, had been food for wild sheep. Bighorns were forced into areas with less food, and as a result, their herds became smaller and less healthy. Domestic sheep also brought diseases into bighorn flocks.

Some biologists think that as many as two million bighorns lived in the American West in the early nineteenth century. Hunting, the loss of mountain grassland, and disease has reduced the bighorn population to 40,000

Left:
Domestic sheep grazing in the Western mountains have been a major problem for wild bighorns.

or less in the late twentieth century. The largest number of remaining bighorns are the approximately 20,000 Rocky Mountain sheep.

Today the bighorn population seems stable. But unlike bison, deer, and elk, bighorns are not recovering quickly from old losses. The spread of lungworm from domestic sheep to bighorns has been a major reason for the bighorn's slow comeback. Another factor lies in the nature of the animal itself. Bighorns do not readily move into new areas and multiply. They tend to stay in small, well-known places. That results in overgrazing and the rapid spread of disease within a flock.

Biologists continue to study the spread of disease from domestic sheep to wild sheep. As greater efforts are made to restrict domestic sheep from bighorn ranges, the bighorn population should increase. More effective methods of restoring bighorns to areas where they no longer exist should also help the sheep.

Meanwhile, broomed horns, lumpy nose, and all, the rowdy bighorn remains a strikingly powerful symbol of the Rocky Mountains.

GLOSSARY

alpine – a mountain location; more specifically, an area above timberline

altitude – the height of an object above the ground

biologist – someone who studies plants and animals

broomed – rough and splintered at the tips

cascades – a series of steep, usually small, waterfalls

cud – food which has been only partially chewed and digested when brought up from the animal's stomach for more thorough chewing

domestic – an animal tamed, raised, and modified by man over a long period of time

dominant – the most powerful

environment – the total surroundings in which a plant or animal lives

ewe – female sheep

extinction – the state of no longer existing

gland – any of several body structures that store and release various liquids

gregarious – sociable; living in the company of others

habitat – a plant or animal's immediate surroundings; its specific, preferred location within the environment

herbivore – a plant-eating animal

hibernation – a deep sleep in which certain animals pass the winter

keratin – horn material

migration – a predictable and seasonal movement from one location to another some distance away

molt – the loss of fur or feathers

odyssey – a long journey

predation – the preying of one animal on another for food

predator – an animal that kills and feeds on other animals

prey – an animal hunted for food by another animal

race – slightly different groups within the same larger group, such as *desert* and *Rocky Mountain* bighorn sheep

rut – the mating season, particularly of horned and antlered animals

species – a group of animals or plants whose members reproduce naturally only with other plants or animals of the same group; a particular kind of animal, such as bighorn sheep

status – position or rank within a group

symbol – something that represents something else

territory – a home area defended by certain animals that live within it

timberline – the height on a mountain at which trees can no longer grow

traditional – that which has been done for generations and has been passed on from one generation to the next

wean – to remove a mammal from a steady diet of mother's milk

INDEX

Numbers in boldface type refer to photo and illustration pages.

47

Rocky Mountain bighorn sheep live in some of the most rugged and remote parts of North America. They also live in rugged, but not-so-remote, mountain parks. There they have become accustomed to people, and often the sheep are quite tame. To these sheep, hikers, autos, and adoring tourists seem more like objects to be viewed with curiosity than with fear. Because park roads and paths often penetrate sheep ranges, a visitor may find bighorns nibbling grass next to the highway, by a cabin, or along the trail. In some national parks, sheep and hikers take midday breaks in the same meadows.

Even in parks, however, finding bighorns is never certain. Their haunts change often with the seasons, and they are capable of quickly bounding into rocky strongholds that are accessible only to them and mountain goats.

Several herds of Rocky Mountain bighorns live on national forest lands in Idaho, Wyoming, Montana, and Colorado. The whereabouts of these herds can usually be obtained from one of the U.S. Forest Service's regional offices in these states.

Bighorn Sites

Banff National Park, Alberta
Denali National Park (Dall's sheep), AK
Glacier National Park, MT
Jasper National Park, Alberta
Kluane National Park (Dall's sheep), Yukon
Kootenay National Park, British Columbia
Rocky Mountain National Park, CO
Waterton Lakes National Park, Alberta
Yellowstone National Park, WY

Ed. Note: Sites listed here so not represent *all* the places where bighorns may be observed. They do represent sites that are reliable and have relatively easy access.